KU-719-747

How to be a Revolutionary Soldier

Written by
Thomas Ratliff

Illustrated by
John James

BOOK HOUSE

Thomas Ratliff studied American History at Central Connecticut State University and the University of Connecticut. He has taught English and history in middle and high school, as well as history and secondary education courses at the college level. He is a co-author of the Matty Trescott series, young adult historical novels set in the Civil War era.

John James was born in London in 1959. He studied at Eastbourne College of Art and has specialized in historical reconstruction since leaving school in 1982. He now lives in Sussex.

Series created and designed by **David Salariya**

Published in Great Britain in 2005 by
Book House, an imprint of
The Salariya Book Company Ltd
25 Marlborough Place, Brighton BN1 1UB

Please visit the Salariya Book Company at:
www.salariya.com

ISBN 1-905087-03-9

A catalogue record for this book is available from the British Library.
Printed and bound in China.

Visit our website at **www.book-house.co.uk**
for free electronic versions of:
You Wouldn't Want To Be An Egyptian Mummy!
You Wouldn't Want To Be A Roman Gladiator!
Avoid joining Shackleton's Polar Expedition!
Avoid sailing on a 19th-century Whaling Ship!

Photographic credits
t=top b=bottom c=centre l=left r=right

The Art Archive / Culver Pictures: 12
The Art Archive / Gunshots: 14
The Art Archive / Gunshots: 20
The Art Archive / Museo Storico Nazionale dell'arte Sanitaria
Rome / Dagli Orti: 25
Boltin Picture Library / Bridgeman Art Library: 29

New York Historical Society / Bridgeman Art Library: 16
New York Historical Society / Bridgeman Art Library: 19
Natham Benn / Corbis: 27
David Muench / Corbis: 10
Richard T. Nowitz / Corbis: 8

Every effort has been made to trace copyright holders. The Salariya Book Company apologises for any unintentional omissions and would be pleased, in such cases, to add an acknowledgement in future editions.

Soldiers Required

How would you like to be a Revolutionary War soldier? The Continental Congress and the Continental Army need you, King George has sent thousands of British soldiers to fight against us in our war for independence. Join General Washington in the fight for freedom!

If you are good with a musket, can ride a horse, and are strong and willing, you will make a good soldier.

Your duties will include:

> Marching and Drilling
> Following Orders
> Setting up Camp
> Standing Guard
> Digging Trenches and Building Fortifications
> Fighting against the British Army

Sign up today and fight for your country!

Contents

How the War Started

The year is 1775, and King George III is the ruler of Great Britain. For many years the British government has governed the American colonies. Recently many Americans have been unhappy with controls over trade and new levels of taxation on items like sugar, glass, paper, and tea. In the city of Boston things have been especially unpleasant. In 1770 a disagreement between citizens and the king's soldiers led to violence, leaving five civilians dead. In 1773 a band of colonists disguised as Native Americans attacked three ships in Boston Harbor, destroying 10,000 pounds of tea. As a result, King George sent troops to Boston to help keep the peace, but relations continued to deteriorate. In April 1775 British troops marched to Lexington and Concord to arrest the colonial leaders—and when the Americans resisted, the first shots for independence were fired.

Sign Up Here

When news of the fighting at Lexington and Concord reaches your hometown, you and your friends decide to sign up to fight against the British. There is no age limit—as long as you are big enough to handle a musket you can sign up. You have the option of joining one of the militia companies in your state or enlisting in the Continental Army, the national army that has been authorized by the Continental Congress meeting in Philadelphia.

Leaving home

▼ Leaving home will not be easy. You have no idea how long you will be gone. Of course, you will miss your family and friends.

Are you ready to serve your country, son?

Dragoon

Foot soldier

Companies

◄ You hope to join an infantry company, and be a foot soldier. Foot soldiers carry muskets as their main weapon. They travel by marching. Other types of companies are artillery (sometimes called matross), responsible for cannons, and cavalry (sometimes called dragoons), soldiers who fight on horseback.

George Washington

◀ George Washington is one of the few men in the colonies with any military background. As a colonel in the colonial militia, Washington served bravely during the French and Indian War. He has a reputation as a brave fighter and gallant leader.

Yes, sir.

Rank of private

▲ If you are accepted you will hold the rank of private, the lowest in the army. You will take orders from an enlisted man with the rank of sergeant. The sergeant reports to a captain who is in charge of the entire company.

American regiments

▲ American regiments vary in size: some have eight companies, while others have as many as 11. A company might have as few as 20 men or as many as 50—most regiments have between 350 and 600 men.

Army Pay

A private gets paid $6.67 a month, although money is scarce and payment is often made in scrip, which is not money but can be turned in for money after the war. One benefit of being a soldier is that your food is supplied for you. In addition you are given other things— tents, blankets, powder and shot for your musket, and a uniform. But since Congress has no power to tax, the states' resources are in short supply throughout most of the war.

Specie

Worthless dollars

When you are paid in cash, it is in Continental dollars. During the war, inflation causes Continental dollars to become almost worthless.

Your lunch, General Washington.

Payment in "specie"

◀ Officers have the same problem as you with the value of the money. You hope to be paid in specie (gold or silver coins) as they don't lose their value. The problem is that Congress does not have any gold or silver to make coins— the only specie in the colonies are issued by the French and Spanish governments.

Ohio Territory

Ohio Territory

◀ After the summer of 1777 Congress does not have enough money to pay the soldiers regularly. The soldiers are promised that at the end of the war they will be paid in full, and many veterans receive 100 acres of land in the Ohio Territory as payment for their years of service.

Thank you.

Washington's war

▲ During the war, General Washington serves without pay, although Congress pays his expenses, which amount to more than $30,000 by the end of the war (several million dollars in today's economy). Washington has a cook and always eats well. His wine bill alone is more than $1,000 a year.

Americans!
Forever bear in mind the BATTLE of LEXINGTON—where British troops, unmolested and unprovoked, wantonly and in a most inhuman manner fired upon and killed a number of our countrymen, then robbed them of their provisions, ransacked, plundered and burned their houses!
Join the Continental Army today!

Newspaper advertisements

▲ To encourage enlistment (and reenlistments), Congress places advertisements in newspapers. Widows and orphans of veterans can qualify for payments that equal a soldier's half-pay for a period of seven years.

Training to Fight

*A*t first your training will be limited to marching and learning to follow orders. You will spend endless days practicing marching in a straight line, loading your musket and firing on command, and learning how to salute and wear your uniform properly. Life in the army is governed by rules and you have to learn them all.

Learning to build

▶ Part of a soldier's training is learning how to build fortifications. For some battles you will dig trenches to fight from or erect breastworks—walls that are about chest high. Most breastworks are made of small trees or fence rails.

What's the password?

▶ When you are serving as a guard, you have to challenge anyone who approaches the camp and wishes to enter. Sometimes the army will use passwords to ensure the safety of the camp.

You're pretty handy with that shovel, Private.

Cannon used in the Second Battle of Saratoga, 1777

General von Steuben

▼ In the winter of 1777–78 a German general, Friedrich Wilhelm Augustus von Steuben, arrives to help General Washington train the troops. The general spoke little or no English when he arrived, but was able to overcome this problem with the help of an interpreter. Under von Steuben's guidance, the Continental Army learns how to manoeuvre under fire, and discipline improves dramatically.

I'd rather be hefting a musket, sir.

Getting organized

▼ General von Steuben begins by training a company of 100 soldiers, then sends them to train other companies. He reorganizes the way that the soldiers live, improving the sanitary conditions in the camp and making the soldiers set their tents in straight rows.

The efforts pay off

In the first battle after von Steuben's arrival, the Continental soldiers are able to defeat the British in a hard-fought struggle at Monmouth, New Jersey. The focus of the war shifts to the south.

Wearing a Uniform

You can tell someone's rank by his uniform: a corporal wears a green stripe on his right shoulder and a sergeant has a red stripe, while officers are distinguished by a cockade, or ribbon, on the front of their hats. Generals wear cockades and also have bright sashes that identify their rank. Officers carry sabers at their sides. Later in the war, the general's sashes are replaced by epaulets (fringed straps or ribbons) on their shoulders.

Redcoats

▼ The British soldiers all wear red jackets and white trousers; it is easy to figure out who the enemy is in the heat of battle.

Can we hold them off, Sergeant?

Blue jackets

▲ Soldiers in the Continental Army wear a uniform that has a blue jacket and white pants. State militia units all have their own uniforms, which vary widely.

Epaulet

American uniforms of the Revolutionary War

Proper apparel

A soldier must have a hat; yours is made of black velvet and is called a cocked hat or tricorn (for the three corners or triangular shape). In addition you will carry a powder horn and a small pouch or cartridge box for lead musket balls. A haversack is slung over your shoulder and holds your personal effects (a tin cup, a pot or plate, mittens for cold weather, brush, razor, and extra socks). You will also carry a knife, fork, and spoon. A canteen made of tin or wood is used to hold water.

As long as our powder lasts!

Black velvet tricorn

Wool jacket

Pewter buttons

Bayonet

Musket

Stockings

Your haversack and its contents

Mug

Cartridge box

Haversack

Canteen

Powder horn

Weapons of War

The average soldier in both armies uses a flintlock musket—a long muzzle-loading weapon that is rather difficult to operate. Your musket has a bayonet, a long, sharp knife that can be fastened to the end of the gun barrel; it is used for close fighting. Sabers are swords worn by officers. Officers use them when giving commands, such as to fire or advance. Sabers are also used in close battle, especially by men on horseback. Some soldiers also carry pistols that fire using the flintlock mechanism.

Brown Bess

The British musket is called a Brown Bess. It weighs almost 12 pounds and fires a one-ounce lead ball up to 250 yards. It has a bayonet and can be loaded and fired three to four times a minute.

Don't take aim, fire!

◄ The Brown Bess is so inaccurate that the British soldiers are trained not to aim, but rather to point in the general direction of the enemy. When an entire unit fires at the same time, the effect of several dozen muskets being discharged can be lethal for the enemy.

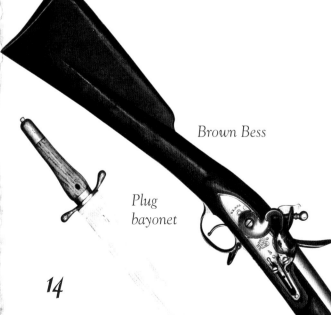

Brown Bess

Plug bayonet

Fixed bayonet

The Brown Bess is even more destructive in a charge—when the bayonet is fixed on the end of the musket it becomes a formidable weapon. It takes a lot of training and discipline to hold your position in the face of an advancing line of British soldiers.

Loading a musket

◄ To load your musket you pour a small amount of powder from your powder horn into the muzzle of the gun.

Then you place a small piece of cloth over the muzzle and put a lead ball on the cloth.

▶ Next you take the ramrod and push the ball and cloth down into the barrel as far as it will go. Finally you pour a tiny amount of powder into the priming pan, located on the side of the weapon next to the hammer.

Take aim and fire!

▶ Cock the hammer, take aim, and fire. A small piece of flint in the hammer will strike the steel plate of the priming pan, causing a spark that will ignite the powder in the pan. This in turn will ignite the powder in the barrel (through a small hole in the barrel), causing the gun to fire.

Army Life

Everything in the army is controlled by rules: everyone acts and dresses the same way. Enlisted men salute officers when they see them, and you must obey orders from anyone who is higher in rank than you. You will be living outdoors much of the time, although living arrangements will vary depending on where you are.

Ready at a moment's notice

▼ Normally you live in a tent, ready to go into battle at a moment's notice. At times you might live in the same place for a while, and have a more permanent (and more comfortable) place to live.

Private from the 1st Georgia Continental Infantry

◄ 19th-century painting by Charles MacKubin Lefferts shows a private loading a charge in his musket.

Winter camp

◄ Armies do not fight during the winter: the weather is too harsh, with snow and ice blocking roads or trails and making it impossible for armies to move around. For the duration of the war, both armies will spend the coldest months in winter quarters—a permanent camp where you will await the coming of spring.

Warmth and comfort

▲ The British often spend their winters in cities like New York or Philadelphia with their soldiers housed in relative comfort and warmth.

Be ready to fight

► In eight years of fighting you will only see about twenty battles, the rest of the time you are going to be encamped, waiting for battle. But you always have to be ready to fight.

Army Food

The Continental Army is supposed to provide each soldier with the following daily rations: a pound of beef or a pound of pork, a pound of bread or flour and three pints of beer. In addition each man gets a gill (four ounces) of rum, as well as milk, tobacco, onions, molasses, chocolate, candles, vinegar, coffee, sugar, and vegetables, and weekly rations of peas or beans, rice or corn meal, and six ounces of butter.

The war lasts eight years, and it is difficult for Congress to raise the money to support the soldiers. There are often shortages, and sometimes food is completely lacking.

Rations

Coffee
Beer
Molasses
Flour
Sugar
Rum
Vinegar
Pork or beef
Milk
Carrots
Potatoes
Candles
Butter
Chocolate
Onions
Tobacco
Peas

The food comes in bulk. Each company receives food for its men, and then the company cook prepares the food. The cooks don't have much training and often the food is boiled until not much flavor is left.

Hardships

◄ In the winter, food is always in short supply. A man who is hungry cannot be expected to fight, and many soldiers are so weak they have to be taken care of by other men or by the camp wives that follow the army. In winter quarters it is common to see men dying of malnutrition, and desertion is also fairly common.

*Private of the
New York Regiment*

Supplies at last

◄ During the winter of 1777–78 the Continental Army will camp at Valley Forge in Pennsylvania. Conditions that winter are especially harsh and more than a quarter of the soldiers die or desert. In late February several wagons and a herd of cattle arrive, courtesy of Jonathan Trumbull, the governor of Connecticut. But even these supplies are not enough to keep the army healthy.

Battle Tactics

The British army is well trained and disciplined, the best fighting force in the world. Its officers are career soldiers, and the enlisted men are kept in line with harsh discipline. Very few Americans have much military experience; the officers only know about warfare from books they have read. But most Americans have experience with guns, either as hunters or frontiersmen protecting their homesteads.

Firing positions

▼ In battle, the British redcoats march into position, forming three rows deep. The first row kneels and fires when commanded to, and then reloads while the second and third rows fire.

Powder horn

In contrast to the British, the American soldiers lack both training and discipline, and in some battles the soldiers become unnerved and run from the approaching British redcoats. It takes a great deal of training to trust your officers and hold your position in battle, especially during a bayonet charge. Early in the war the Americans lose many battles due to a lack of discipline among the troops, especially the volunteers, who make up the majority of the soldiers.

Professional soldiers

◄ British generals are professional soldiers with years of experience. They are well versed in the art of war and understand battle strategy and tactics much better than do the American officers, most of whom are volunteers with no real military training.

Hat

Haversack

Musket

Sword

► The British soldiers carry packs that weigh as much as 100 pounds. A long day of marching or fighting is exhausting. The Continental soldiers are able to move faster and can retreat quickly when needed. In this way, General Washington avoids losing his army; if a battle is going badly he can simply pull back, preserving his army to fight another day. Washington only wins a few of the battles he engages in, but by keeping his army in the field he keeps the war going.

Revolutionary War Women

During the war some of the married men bring their wives along, and the women help the soldiers in many ways. Some help to cook meals; others repair damaged uniforms; and many help to tend the sick and wounded. A few women get involved in the fighting. One such woman is Mary Hays McCauley. Better known as Molly Pitcher, Mary followed her husband to war, spending the winter with his artillery corps at Valley Forge and the following summer at the Battle of Monmouth Courthouse.

Reload men!

Molly Pitcher

▼ Mary risked her life repeatedly to carry pitchers of water to the exhausted and thirsty men. When she encountered a wounded man on the field of battle, she picked him up and carried him to safety.

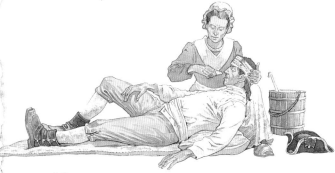

In combat

▲ When Mary's husband was wounded she stepped in and helped the gun crew fire their cannon. For her bravery, General Washington issued a proclamation making Mary an official member of his army with the rank of sergeant.

Deborah Sampson

▶ Other women also contribute to the war effort. The best known is Deborah Sampson. At the age of 21 she decided to fight for her country. Deborah disguised herself as a man and enlisted as Robert Shurtleff in May 1782.

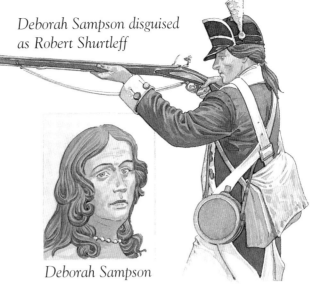

Deborah Sampson disguised as Robert Shurtleff

Deborah Sampson

Wounded in battle

▲ Deborah was wounded in battle, a bruise to her head that she let a doctor treat and a bullet wound in the leg that she treated herself so as not to be discovered. She removed a lead ball from her leg using a pocketknife and a needle. As a result, her identity was protected for a few more months. But her leg never healed properly and for the rest of her life she walked with a limp. After the war Deborah received a soldier's pension. She married, had three children, and lived to be 66.

Working women

▶ Thousands of other women supported the war effort by working the family farms while their husbands were off fighting. Without this valuable contribution, the Continental Army would not have lasted even one year.

Battlefield Injuries

During the war, the number of killed and wounded is not terribly high. Muskets are not that accurate and there are few battles where there is hand-to-hand fighting. American battle casualties are very light. Of 200,000 American soldiers, only 4,435 are killed and another 6,354 are wounded. But almost 20,000 die of disease, exposure to the elements, or starvation.

"Sawbones"

▼ Most doctors have little medical training, and surgeons (who remove bullets and perform amputations) have no training whatsoever. The surgeons are called "sawbones" by the soldiers.

Drastic Measures

▼ Amputation is one treatment that a surgeon can provide that is effective.

I'm afraid that we have to amputate your leg.

Few medicines

Only a few medicines are available to doctors. The most common treatment is to bleed a patient who is sick or wounded, in the belief that bad blood is a cause of illness or infection. Unfortunately this practice leaves the patient weakened and less able to fight off the disease or to heal properly.

Biggest killers

▶ Smallpox, influenza, and cholera, the biggest killers of the war, are more common in summer. There are few doctors in the Continental Army, and the only nurses are the soldiers' wives.

Hold him steady!

Survivors

▼ Many lives are saved by amputation, although survivors are often left with little to do but beg for a living.

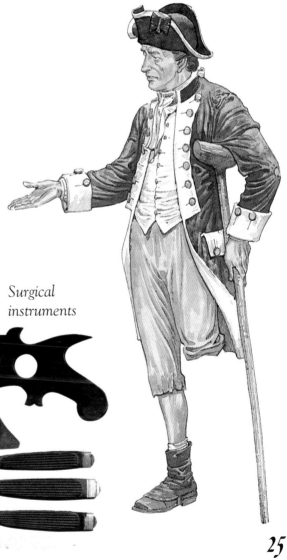

Surgical instruments

Earning a Promotion

Promotions are available for men who prove themselves in battle. Unfortunately sometimes advancement comes because a sergeant or corporal is killed or captured and someone is promoted to fill the position. With rank comes responsibility and you are expected to show leadership and courage in battle.

Badge of Honor

During the war, General Washington creates two badges of distinction to be worn on the uniform.

Promotion

▲ Being promoted won't change your life very much. But it might mean more privilege or better living quarters, as well as respect from your fellow soldiers.

Survivors lead

If nothing else, a promotion means you have survived the battles you have been in, and that fact alone will give the other men confidence in you.

▶ The first badge is called the Badge of Military Merit. This badge, a heart figure on a purple ribbon, is given to soldiers noted for outstanding service or bravery.

A soldier who wears the Badge of Military Merit is recognized as a hero. He can pass guards and sentinels without being challenged. This badge eventually becomes known as the Purple Heart (which is earned by a soldier who is wounded in battle).

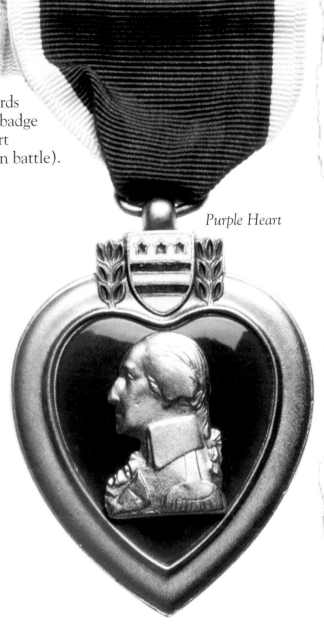

Purple Heart

The chevron

The second badge is a chevron, a V-shaped stripe to be worn on the left sleeve, that signifies three years of honorable service. By the end of the war, you and several of your fellow soldiers will have two chevrons for your six-plus years of service.

Can You Get the Top Job?

George Washington is the commander in chief of the Continental Army. It is difficult for an enlisted man to receive a promotion to the level of officer and nearly impossible for a lieutenant to be promoted all the way to the rank of general. Officers are usually men who are wealthy and well educated. Even though many Americans hope to create a country that is free of European ideas of social class, there is a division in the army that separates most enlisted men from the officers.

The Yorktown peninsula

▼ The combined army under the French general Jean-Baptiste Rochambeau and Washington, 16,000 men, moves south and lays siege to the Yorktown peninsula.

Hold your fire, boys...

American Independence

◄ In September 1783 the Treaty of Paris officially ends the Revolutionary War. The British recognize American independence and agree to evacuate all soldiers from the former colonies. The Treaty of Paris grants the Americans independence and gives them all lands east of the Mississippi River, except New Orleans and the land now known as Florida.

Cornwallis is stranded

The French fleet under Admiral Francois de Grasse sails north from the West Indies to intercept the British. A great sea battle drives off the English ships and General Charles Cornwallis is stranded.

...they are surrendering!

Surrender

▲ At the same time American and French sappers (men who dig tunnels and trenches) are busy. They dig trenches toward the British line and are able to move their cannons closer and closer. Without the British fleet to help him escape, Cornwallis realizes that his army is doomed. On October 19, 1781 he surrenders to George Washington.

When the fighting is over

▲ The war is over! In American cities church bells ring out in celebration. After years of fighting, you will finally go home to your family farm in Connecticut.

Eagle and flag

◄ The American symbol of the bald eagle with the Stars and Stripes (*left*) is adopted by Congress in 1782.

Your Interview

Answer these questions to test your knowledge, then look at page 32 to find out if you have what it takes to get the job.

Q1 How will you spend your first few months in the army?
A reading
B fighting
C training

Q2 How much will you earn as a private?
A $6.67 a month
B $28.00 a week
C $1,000 a year

Q3 Who is commander in chief of the Continental Army?
A General Howe
B General Washington
C General Rochambeau

Q4 What is the British soldier's musket called?
A Brown Betty
B Brown Bess
C Brown Susan

Q5 Who reorganizes the Continental Army and brings discipline to the soldiers?
A General Burgoyne
B Governor Trumbull
C General von Steuben

Q6 How many years do you have to serve to earn a V-shaped patch on the left sleeve of your uniform?
A six months
B three years
C five years

Q7 What are the three types of units in the Continental Army?
A infantry, artillery, and matross
B artillery, dragoons, and swordsmen
C infantry, artillery, and cavalry

Q8 What is the name of the special voucher you receive for pay?
A military money
B American dollars
C scrip

Q9 What bonus might you receive at the end of the war?
A 100 dollars
B 100 acres of land
C 100 pounds of beef

Q10 In what year did the Revolutionary War begin?
A 1775
B 1770
C 1776

Glossary

Artillery. Cannons.

Badge of Military Merit. A military award for heroism.

Breastworks. A fortification made of logs or earth.

Cavalry. Soldiers who fight on horseback (also known as dragoons).

Cholera. A sometimes fatal intestinal disease caused by contaminated water or food.

Continental Army. Colonial army formed by the Continental Congress to fight against the British.

Continental Congress. The government of the colonies (and after 1776 the newly formed states).

Dragoons. Soldiers who fight on horseback (also called cavalry).

Fortifications. Trenches, breastworks, or other structures erected to protect an army in the field.

French and Indian War. A war between France and England (1754–63) that involved the colonists and their Native American allies—also known in Europe as the Seven Years' War (where it lasted from 1756 to 1763).

Haversack. A linen or cotton bag used to carry a soldier's personal gear.

Infantry. Soldiers trained to fight on foot (also called foot soldiers).

Inflation. A situation when the value of money decreases.

Influenza. Viral infection of the respiratory tract (also known as the flu).

Matross. Another name for artillery or cannons.

Monmouth Courthouse, Battle of. A battle in northern New Jersey in June 1778.

Ohio Territory. Land that became the state of Ohio.

Pewter. Metal made from tin, copper, and lead.

Priming pan. Part of a flintlock used to ignite the powder charge in a musket.

Sapper. A soldier who digs trenches or tunnels.

Scrip. Paper used as a substitute for money.

Smallpox. A contagious disease caused by a pox virus.

Specie. Gold or silver coins.

Treaty of Paris. Treaty signed in September 1783 that ended the American Revolution.

Valley Forge. Winter quarters (1777–78) for the Continental Army.

Winter quarters. Permanent camp set up in which an army may spend the winter.

Yorktown, Battle of. Last battle of the Revolutionary War.

Index

Further Reading

Schanzer, Roslyn. *George vs. George: The American Revolution as Seen from Both Sides.* National Geographic, 2004.

Murray, Stuart. *American Revolution.* (Eyewitness Books). Dorling Kindersley, 2005.

Have You Got the Job?

Count up your correct answers (*below right*) and find out if you got the job.

Your score:

10 Congratulations! You are going to make a great soldier.

8–9 Almost ready to be a soldier.

6–7 You show promise—we will remember your name.

4–5 Not quite ready for the army.

Fewer than 4 You will have to try harder if you want to join the Continental Army.

Q10 (A) page 5
Q9 (B) page 9
Q8 (C) page 8
Q7 (C) page 6
Q6 (B) page 26

Q5 (C) page 11
Q4 (B) pages 14–15
Q3 (B) page 28
Q2 (A) page 8
Q1 (C) page 10